ROBBIE FOWLER

HEROES

First published in 1997 by
Invincible Press
an imprint of HarperCollins*Publishers*
London

A CIP catalogue record for this book is available from the British Library.

ISBN 0 00 218821 X

Created and produced by Flame Tree Publishing,
a part of The Foundry Creative Media Company Ltd,
The Long House, Antrobus Road,
Chiswick, London W4 5HY.

Thanks to Jim Drewett, Alex Leith and the Deadline squad
for their help in researching this book.

ROBBIE FOWLER

HEROES

Introduction by Robert Jeffery

Main text by Philip Dodd

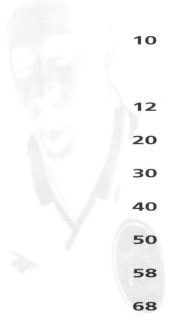

**MAYBE IT WAS** a quiet news day, but the back pages were full of only one thing: Robbie Fowler was the new kid in town.

On a Tuesday night in October 1993, Fowler – just 18 years old and with only a handful of first team appearances under his belt – scored not once, but five times as Liverpool crushed Fulham in the League Cup. He had gained his first goal in the League only days earlier, yet now he was on fire: many fans could not remember a more promising performance. Those who did spoke of Keegan, Rush and Toshack.

Many had seen it coming for quite some time: Fowler had blasted his way through the Anfield youth team and reserves in a flurry of instinctive and often spectacular goals since turning professional little more than a year earlier. Clearly, he was marked out for greatness.

Robert Bernard Fowler was born in the notoriously rough Toxteth area of Liverpool on 9 April 1975. From an early age it was clear that he had an uncanny aptitude for football: he was turning out for Liverpool schoolboys by the time he was in his teens and, despite being a boyhood Everton fan by virtue of his father, signed for the red half of Merseyside on a YTS scheme as soon as he turned 16.

Graeme Souness blooded his young prodigy early and was not to be disappointed: under the guiding hand of the legendary Ian Rush, his first season saw him bang in 12 goals in 28 games. For an 18-year-old it was a terrifyingly fast start to a career in Premiership football.

Fowler – despite the presence of more experienced first class strikers at the club – quickly became Rush's partner of choice up front. He matured fast and effectively as the Reds licked their wounds at again missing out in the title race, taking the Coca-Cola Cup by way of consolation.

By the time Souness was succeeded by Roy Evans, Fowler was widely regarded as the most prodigious striker of his generation. His full England call-up came in January 1996, and he made his debut as a sub against Bulgaria two months later. Though Shearer and Sheringham were the preferred choices for Euro 96, they were more than aware of the awesome goal-grabber on the bench; a player with a natural instinct only found in the true greats, able to create something out of nothing and possessing the pace, guile and natural ability to outwit any opponent.

Perhaps it was an incident in the 1996-97 season which best illustrated the measure of the man. Against Arsenal he appealed for a penalty not to be given against David Seaman for pulling him down. It brought delight from critics and fans, but that's Robbie Fowler – international superstar, but just a modest lad from Toxteth deep down.

***Robert Jeffery***

## THE TOXTETH TERROR

**IT USED** TO BE SAID there were three classic ways for a young lad to escape from an inner-city upbringing. You could prove yourself the hard way by being pretty nifty with a pair of boxing gloves. You could join a rock'n'roll band. Or you could play professional football. A kick-about in the local backstreets with a tennis ball, some spirited performances on the school soccer team and with luck on your side you might catch the eye of a talent scout for one of the big clubs.

Robbie Fowler is living proof of the theory. He was born in the Toxteth district of Liverpool, which became lodged for right or wrong in the public memory as a tough, uncompromising, disadvantaged area following the riots of the early 1980s; an urban powder keg right up there with Brixton and Manchester's Moss Side.

**GROWING UP** in the heart of Liverpool imposes one critical, inescapable choice: to be a Liverpool or an Everton fan. Robbie's father was an Evertonian and not unnaturally that was Robbie's early preference. But since then Robbie has become an Anfield hero – and his father has gamely and pragmatically attended nearly every match in which his son has worn a Liverpool shirt.

Like Steve McManaman, another Scouser in a team in which local players are rare, Robbie is as genuinely Liverpudlian as the Mersey, the Cavern and the Kop.

*I used to run wherever the ball was. I'd be in the back four, midfield, attack – all in the same game! I just wanted to be on the ball all the time and get involved.*
Robbie Fowler on his schoolboy days, *Total Football*, 1995

**ROBERT BERNARD FOWLER** was born on 9 April 1975 in Toxteth. His team-mate and friend Steve McManaman, three years older than Robbie, was brought up in the Kirkdale district of Liverpool (Jason McAteer, hailing from Birkenhead, is deemed by true Scousers to have been born just beyond the pale).

With a family tradition of Everton support, Robbie's boyhood footballing heroes were Goodison Park favourites like Graeme Sharp and Trevor Steven (he also admired the skills of Diego Maradona). But despite this early preference in one of football's most divisive derby rivalries, once he had made the decision to sign at Anfield, just half a mile or so away across Stanley Park, he had to transfer loyalties.

*When I was little, I loved Everton and went everywhere to see them. I would probably still be supporting them if I wasn't playing football.*
Robbie Fowler, *Total Football*, 1995

**PLAYING IN THE STREET,** Robbie, as kids tend to do, would keep up a running commentary on the game in progress, taking on the role of Graeme Sharp, now in management with Oldham. Sharp can now return the compliments.

*He's got all-round talent, a great eye for a chance, and his finishes are not just impressive they are often exceptional.*
Graeme Sharpe, *The Observer*, 1996

*I suppose all the boys here want to be another Fowler.*
*He's a real Toxy boy – works hard at his game.*
Harry Hudson, Liverpool fan, *FourFourTwo*, 1996

**HIS PROMISE** was spotted early. With the encouragement
of his father, Robbie Snr, and the benevolent patronage of
Bob Lynch, a schoolteacher who managed the Liverpool
Schoolboys side, his natural skill was allowed to flourish.

*Young players get a bad name these days. They've got money*
*to burn and usually the old connections go up in flames as*
*soon as they start getting their names in the papers. But not*
*Robert. He's a Toxteth boy through and through. He's got to*
*be worth his weight in gold to Liverpool but you'd never*
*know it by the way he reacts. He still calls me 'sir' and rings*
*me at least a couple of times a week.*
Bob Lynch, manager of Liverpool Schools Under-14 side, *FourFourTwo*, 1996

**ROBBIE** became a Liverpool trainee at the age of 11, and
proof that he had successfully severed the Everton connection
came with his decision to sign Schoolboy forms with Liverpool
at 14, even though he could have transferred to the youth
scheme at Goodison Park at 14 if he'd wanted to.

Throughout Robbie's career, Liverpool greats of earlier
generations have helped and encouraged him. It was Kenny
Dalglish who secured his signature, and reportedly Dalglish
always insisted he had the young Fowler on his side during
the regular five-a-side games which formed part of practice
sessions at Liverpool's Melwood training ground.

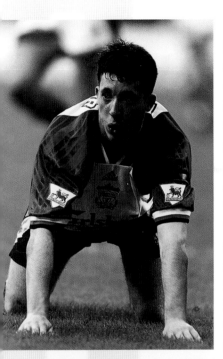

Signing as a YTS trainee in 1991, Robbie continued his commitment to the club that was now taking a big stake in his future. He also came under the influence of 1970s Kop star Steve Heighway, now the youth development director at Anfield, who was responsible for overseeing the successful transition from promising schoolboy to fully fledged professional, and who also nurtured the talent of Steve McManaman, coming up through the ranks at the same time.

*His father just left Robbie in our hands. I think he took the view that if his son was content at Liverpool, then he was content.*
**Steve Heighway, *The Observer*, 1996**

**IN APRIL 1992,** the year after he'd signed as a YTS trainee, he turned pro. It was his 17th birthday. Dalglish having quit suddenly and emotionally as Liverpool manager in 1991, Fowler would make his debut under another loyal club servant, Graeme Souness. Robbie knew that the Anfield 'family' had high hopes for him, and he didn't want to let them down.

*You get a lot of players who train and work really hard and they're told that they're not good enough. I was quite fortunate 'cos I worked on my game and I wasn't a bad player so I was given a chance.*
Robbie Fowler, *FourFourTwo*, 1996

*I've known him since he was 14, and I can honestly say his progress in the last six years has not been a surprise. It was obvious from the word go that he was going to be prolific.*
Alan Hansen, *The Observer*, 1996

## MAKING HIS MARK

**WHEN HE** FIRST CAME into the senior Liverpool team, Robbie Fowler was not a completely unknown quantity to sports writers and pundits. He already made an impression as the top scorer in the England side which had won a European Under-18 tournament during the summer of 1993, and so it was widely expected that he would soon be given the opportunity to make an appearance in a Liverpool first team shirt.

The Liverpool that Fowler was joining was in a slump by their own high standards. Graeme Souness had taken over as manager in April 1991, tasked with the job of returning the club to the glory days of the previous decades. At the end of the 1991 season, defeat by Nottingham Forest in their last match had handed the title to Arsenal.

In 1991-92 they'd won the FA Cup but come a poor sixth in the League (their first time out of the Top 2 for eleven years), and the following season the club had failed in Europe, been dumped out of the Coca-Cola Cup by Palace, surrendered their defence of the FA Cup to Bolton, and finished sixth again in the Premiership.

The beginning of the new 1993-94 season did not look promising: losing four of their first five matches, including a defeat at Goodison Park, and the unsavoury spectacle of team-mates Grobbelaar and McManaman indulging in fisticuffs on the pitch. *What on earth has happened to the dignity and discipline that were the hallmarks of the great Anfield teams*? asked *The Sun*. Liverpool had been going through a bit of a goal drought, but Robbie Fowler, untainted and undaunted, was about to turn on the tap.

The first chance for Robbie to prove what he could do was in a Coca-Cola Cup second round, first leg tie against Fulham in September 1993. He began in style, providing the centres for two goals and scoring the third in a 3-1 victory.

*Last night, as thunder rumbled, lightning forked and rain teemed, Liverpool found the enthusiasm which had deserted them at Everton on Sunday.... They even found a hero of sorts, the 18-year-old Robbie Fowler, who seized his initial chance of first-team football with verve and alacrity. Any reluctance to accord him full heroic status stemmed from recognition of the fact that he probably meets stiffer defences playing for Liverpool reserves.*

**David Lacey, *The Guardian*, September 1993**

**LATER IN** THE MONTH he was able to make his first League appearance against Chelsea, although his first League goal had to wait a little longer, until a strike against Oldham in October. But in between he had already achieved one record-breaking feat: in the second leg of the Coca-Cola tie with Fulham, Fowler claimed all five Liverpool goals in the Reds' 5-0 victory.

It was only the fourth time a Liverpool player had scored five goals in a match – the others were Andy McGuigan in 1902, John Evans in 1954 and Ian Rush in 1983 – and the first to do so in a cup match. Even more significantly, no other Liverpool player had managed to get a look-in on the scoresheet: one match reporter described Ian Rush's contribution to the match as *anonymous in comparison*. With this single-handed demolition job, Robbie had arrived with a serious bang in only his fourth senior game.

*It could have been six but for a flying save by Stannard to tip over his superb chip two minutes from time. At the end of the game he had rocketed himself to the top of the club's scoring charts.... On this evidence there will be more to come. The irony was that Fowler was the only Liverpool player on the pitch last night who didn't cost the club a penny.*
**Richard Tanner, *The Mirror*, October 1993**

*It'd be easy to go overboard about Robbie, and I don't want to do that yet. But he's clearly going to be very special. Anyone who's seen our reserves in the past two years would know that he threatens to score whenever he plays. He's like Rushie, always there or thereabouts in the box. Now everyone's going to know his name. It's up to him to come to terms with that, and our job to help him cope.*
**Graeme Souness, *The Independent*,
October 1993**

**THE NEXT MONTH** Fowler got his call-up to the England Under-21 team, making his debut against San Marino, and scored three in a 4-2 win at home against Southampton. High-scoring contributions to Liverpool scorelines were becoming something of a habit. He had made himself almost immediately into a first team regular, and he was still only 18.

*Those five goals were at the start of my career and I was dead shy. I didn't really know what was happening. The time I realised I was famous was when I'd go shopping and that, and people were staring at me. Or you'd go out for a drink and people would come up and ask for autographs, which is a bit annoying if you're out with your mates or a girlfriend. You can't relax.*

**Robbie Fowler,**
*Total Football*, **1995**

**AT THE END** of his first season as a professional, Robbie had scored 18 goals in 33 appearances, a strike rate of 55 per cent; his League tally had been 12 goals from 28 appearances. The Fowler goal haul was the same as Ian Rush's, even though Robbie had missed two months of the season after incurring a stress-fracture of the leg against Bristol City.

Perhaps most telling was the manner in which he had come back from that injury. It was the return match in the Merseyside derby, and Robbie avenged Liverpool's defeat by Everton earlier in the season by scoring the winner in a 2-1 victory. In future years Fowler would recall that as one of his most memorable goals: in the hothouse of a Merseyside derby, against his former favourite club and in his very first season. The big match flair and temperament were already there to see.

## THE STRIKERS CLUB

**FOLLOWING** GRAEME SOUNESS'S departure as Liverpool manager in January 1994, the 1994-95 season was Roy Evans' first full season in charge. It was a season that allowed the relationship between Robbie Fowler and Ian Rush to mature, giving the youngster the perfect opportunity to watch and learn from the Anfield legend's wiles and experience. He was able to enhance his innate goalscoring instincts – Alan Hansen described him as *the best in the country by a mile* – with additional qualities to improve his all-round performance: chasing down the ball, defending from the front (an Ian Rush speciality), intelligent, selfless support play. Comparing Rush and Fowler, commentators noted that Robbie generally ran with the ball more than his mentor, and was able to benefit from a higher level of unpredictability. Defences *knew* what Rush would do, they just couldn't stop him doing it, whereas Fowler simply bamboozled them into submission.

*I did have a spell at left-midfield at one stage, when I was at school, but I decided I loved to see the net rattling. That's me all over. So, upfront it was.*
**Robbie Fowler, *Total Football*, 1995**

**30**

**THROUGHOUT** his career, Fowler has always been quick to acknowledge the role Ian Rush has played in his development.

*The way I play ... I mean you need help, Rushie was always there to help me out, you know in a positional sense or whatever.... Probably everything I know I've learnt off Ian Rush.*
**Robbie Fowler,** *FourFourTwo,* **1996**

*Ian may be a good teacher, but Robbie's a good learner.*
**Roy Evans**

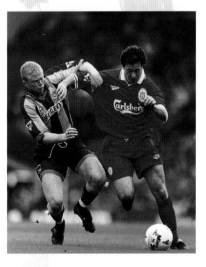

**IT WAS** fitting that in January 1996, when the recently honoured Ian Rush MBE came on in a sixth-round tie against Rochdale to beat Denis Law's FA Cup goalscoring record, the pass creating the opening was gallantly laid on for him by Fowler. Rush returned the favour when he presented Robbie with his second consecutive PFA Young Player of the Year trophy in the spring, announcing the winner as 'My son, Robbie Fowler', making clear the heritage that was passing from one generation to the next.

*I leave Liverpool in good hands. Robbie will probably eclipse all that I have achieved at Liverpool.*
Ian Rush

*What Ian has achieved at Liverpool, I don't think will ever be beaten. I would be happy to achieve half of it.*
Robbie Fowler, *Total Football*, 1995

**RUSH'S RECORD** is some target: he is the top scorer of all time in both the FA and League Cups, has scored more goals in cup finals than any other player, and holds the Liverpool record for goals in a single season (47 in all competitions). Only Roger Hunt scored more goals for Liverpool. But if Robbie Fowler stays with Liverpool, who knows...?

Fowler began his second season in the Liverpool team with panache, breaching the parsimonious Arsenal defence three times in 4 minutes and 33 seconds – a Premiership record. 'WOWLER!' screamed the headline in *The Sun*.

*Fowler was a mere 93 secs from rewriting the record books for the fastest post-war hat-trick scored in the top division. But that statistic alone does not tell the full story. In the first half, Fowler made 16 passes and every last one was successful. Sixteen passes to 16 red shirts – it should enter the record books along with the details of his five minutes of glory in front of his native Scousers.*
Martin Samuel, *The Sun*, August 1994

*Arsenal are probably one of the best defensive sides in the country so to score three is brilliant. I missed one against them last season, so it makes up for that.*
**Robbie Fowler**

**AT THE OTHER** end of the season he helped Liverpool win the Coca-Cola Cup with Liverpool, beating Bolton 2-1 at Wembley. In the second leg of the Reds' semi-final against Crystal Palace, Fowler, who had scored the only goal in the first leg at Anfield, sealed Palace's fate, and secured Liverpool's place at Wembley with, again, the only goal in a tight match – a 27th minute shot from close range.

He ended the season having scored 31 goals in 57 appearances, including 25 League goals in 42 League appearances, and was only pipped to the golden boot award in the Premiership by Alan Shearer – as it was, Robbie's mid-season had been, set against his usual prolific yardstick, a touch flat. But it was little surprise when he was named PFA Young Player of the Year in May 1995.

His second season at Anfield had helped him to develop and stabilise his talents, proving that his knack for goalscoring was no flash in the pan, and to observe other members of the goalscoring club at close quarters.

Fowler had become a strong admirer of Alan Shearer, especially his work rate for the rest of the team, and Jürgen Klinsmann, Les Ferdinand and Ian Wright had also caught his eye. He was particularly pleased, he told one reporter, that there were more and more English forwards becoming household names.

*I don't think any forward can tell you how to score goals. It comes natural. I've been scoring goals since I was 11 years old. So it's easy. Being in the right place at the right time is the best answer, I suppose.*
Robbie Fowler, *Total Football*, 1995

**FOR THE START** of the 1995-96 season, another striker joined the Liverpool squad. Stan Collymore arrived from Nottingham Forest as Britain's most expensive player and, while the new boy was being given time to develop a partnership with Ian Rush, Fowler was relegated to the bench for the first matches of the season. He wasn't sidelined for too long, though: an injury to Collymore gave him the chance to force his way back in.

The teenager, already valued with a £10 million price tag – not that Liverpool had any intention of selling his talents to any of their rivals – had learnt his lesson after being dropped from the opening two games of the season. However brilliant his strikes, he could not become complacent.

*I needed a kick up the backside because in hindsight I was taking my place for granted and that is something you should never do at Liverpool.*
Robbie Fowler, *The Mirror*, 1996

## CAP, CUP AND KOP

**WHEN STAN COLLYMORE'S** INJURY problems gave Robbie the chance to regain his place in the first team, he let his scoring do the talking in the new 1995-96 season. Bolton Wanderers watched four Fowler goals go past them in one match. Arsenal experienced the Fowler hat-trick effect again – even if this time it took him slightly longer than 4 minutes and 33 seconds. He even put four past the mighty Manchester United during that season's two League encounters, including one stunning free-kick at Anfield just before Christmas, when his strike over a six-man United wall left Peter Schmeichel rooted to the spot, a game which included his 50th goal in Premiership football. The 1995-96 campaign would be Fowler's second consecutive thirty-something season, ending the season with 36 goals to his name in all appearances, and 28 Premiership goals.

As the Euro 96 campaign drew near, England's management team could concentrate on the likely shape of the team, free of worries about qualifying, since they were guaranteed a place in the final as hosts of the tournament.

Robbie's claim for consideration was underlined by a gripping match at Anfield against Manchester United in October 1995, memorable as the match when Eric Cantona made his return to top-flight football following the eight-month suspension imposed for his infamous kung fu kick at Selhurst Park the previous season.

Fowler was outstanding: after Cantona had set up United's opening goal for Nicky Butt, Robbie responded with two strikes. The match was drawn when Cantona equalised with a penalty. But on the big stage, against the best in the country, and arguably the best in the world, he had yet again delivered.

*You ask anyone at the club –*
*I never, ever get nervous.*
**Robbie Fowler, *Goal*, 1995**

*What impresses me about Robbie is that he expects to score a goal from every two chances. That is an old-fashioned goalscorer's attitude, one you don't see too often and something now sadly missing from the modern game.*
**Jimmy Greaves, *The Sun*, 1996**

**AGAINST ASTON VILLA,** in the FA Cup semi-final at Old Trafford in March, Fowler guaranteed Liverpool's passage to the final with two goals: the first magnificent diving header eclipsed only by his superb volley in the second half.

*He often shoots early, he doesn't mind where he shoots from, but he seems to get late fade on his shots like a golfer. He usually gets ten out of ten shots on target, and with nine out of ten he hits the corners. If he is doing that deliberately, his accuracy is quite amazing.*
Villa keeper, Mark Bosnich, *The Observer,* 1996

**BUT THE GOALS** that Robbie chose to remember were not necessarily the spectacular strikes that the fans relished. When asked about his most memorable goal in an interview, he responded:

*The goal that springs to mind, I don't think anyone knows it because it – 'scuse my language – it was a crap goal, against Leeds at Elland Road. We won 2-0, it was 1-0 at the time. One of the defenders had sort of backheaded it and I ran onto it in the box and sidefooted it past the keeper. It was a stupid goal, but in my eyes it was a good goal.*

Robbie Fowler, *FourFourTwo*, 1996

The spring of 1996 was a busy period

for Robbie Fowler. On 16 March, marking his landmark 100th League game for Liverpool, against Chelsea, he headed home from a Jason McAteer cross in the second half – his 30th for the season. In the same month he scored the first two goals in the 4-3 equally nail-biting re-run of the 4-3 nail-biter against Newcastle the previous season.

And in the space of a few precious days he scored those two goals against Aston Villa in the 3-0 win which took Liverpool to the FA Cup Final at Wembley (where they lost, disappointingly, to Eric Cantona's decisive volley), and enjoyed his first full England cap.

*All my life I have wanted to play in the FA Cup Final
and for England. It has happened in the space of a week –
it's just unbelievable.*
Robbie Fowler, *The Sun*, April 1996

Earlier in the year rumours that an Irish family connection might have been forthcoming if an England call-up was denied had been smartly dismissed by Fowler: *I've always wanted to play for England, full stop.*

*He is exciting, he is dangerous, he frightens defenders. He takes the responsibility to be the main goalscorer and he appears to relish the pressure. I hope he gets the chance to play a game for England. He deserves it.*
Jimmy Greaves, *The Sun*, January 1996

*He has got to force out some very formidable names, the competition in the front area is very finely balanced and has been for some time. It is all very well wondering why he has not been in sooner, but who am I to leave out?*
Terry Venables, *The Sun*, January 1996

**ROBBIE** had indeed been called up for England's pre-Euro 96 get-together at Bisham Abbey (arriving belatedly with Stan Collymore) before the Euro year in January. His first full international appearance came against the 1994 World Cup semi-finalists Bulgaria on 27 March 1996, when he was brought on as a substitute for Alan Shearer – Robbie didn't touch the ball much, but he had achieved his ambition (*I was very comfortable and pleased with not being nervous*, he said afterwards). Subsequently he would make a full appearance against Croatia, due to be one of the Euro 96 contenders, and came on as substitute against China on England's infamous pre-tournament Far East tour.

The Observer reported the rumour of a media bandwagon to get Fowler a secure place in England's Euro team. The paper's view was that he didn't need any outside help, but that Alan Shearer was still clearly the leading marksman for the moment. Robbie's time could come.

*I don't think international football will be any problem to Robbie at all. He keeps asking me for one of my old shirts, but I'm planning to ask for one of his.*
Graeme Sharp, *The Observer*, 1996

## SINNER TO SAINT

**AS FOOTBALL** MADE ITS WAY home, Fowler was only able to make a limited impact on Euro 96, while Alan Shearer, Paul Gascoigne and Teddy Sheringham took all the goalscoring plaudits.

He came off the bench in England's first round 4-1 win against Holland, and was also a substitute in the quarter-final victory over Spain. David Seaman's heart-stopping, match-winning save from Miguel Angel Nadal saved Robbie the pleasure/pain of taking the next penalty kick.

If he hadn't been able to play as high profile a part in England's campaign as he and his fans would have liked, overall 1995-96 had been a good season for Robbie Fowler: he had picked up the PFA Young Player of the Year trophy again, only the second player after Ryan Giggs to win the award in consecutive seasons. He had gained his first cap, and appeared in the FA Cup Final. And by the end of that season, he and Stan Collymore had forged a good and, for Liverpool, a lucrative front partnership.

He had also gone some way to ridding himself of a reputation as a bit of a lad, the scally's scally, a young hellraiser who could too easily forget his public responsibilities.

It hadn't been any one particular incident, more a gradual build-up over a year or so of – often frankly juvenile – bad behaviour.

In October 1994 he had been sent off during an England Under-21 international in Austria after 88 minutes for swearing. At the time he was on a seemingly unstoppable path to a full cap. The four-match UEFA ban cannot have hurt as much as the realisation that he had done serious damage to his aspirations at the international level.

That same year, he received a carpeting from the Liverpool management for indiscreet, though doubtless tongue-in-cheek, comments he had made about sex and beer (aka booze and shagging) in Loaded, and the following February he was rapped by the FA for baring his backside to Leicester City fans during Liverpool's Boxing Day encounter against the Foxes. He was fined £1000 and 'rested' by manager Roy Evans.

In September 1995, on an England Under-21 trip to Portugal, the hotel room he was sharing with Kevin Gallen and Trevor Sinclair was damaged, so Robbie found himself up before the FA again, with some more explaining to do. He should have paid more attention to what he had told *The Sun* in a feature immediately before the Portugal game:

*Robbie Fowler will have two missions when he steps out against Portugal here tonight. The Liverpool hitman is aiming to shoot England's Under-21s to the quarter finals of the European Championship AND prove he has lost his hothead tag.*
**The Sun**

*Fowler, 20, was sent off when he last played for the Under-21s – against Austria – and served a four-match UEFA ban for abusive language. 'What I did that night was stupid. It will never happen again.'*
**The Sun**, September 1995

**EVEN MORE** recklessly, Robbie found himself involved in a public scrap at an airport with Liverpool hard man Neil Ruddock during a UEFA Cup trip to Russia the same month. The incident resulted from a Fowler prank involving some shoes purchased by Mrs Ruddock. There were reports of blood in the check-in area.

*If Razor had hit me properly I don't think I'd have been
around to talk about it!*
**Robbie Fowler, *The Mirror*, 1996**

**THE REST** of the 1995-96 season saw a concerted attempt
by Robbie, or the Liverpool spin doctors, to portray him as a
reformed, responsible member of the footballing community.
The tearaway, wild child image was abandoned; the laddish
prankster consigned to the bin. It was goodbye to the Robbie
Fowler who had returned from his summer holidays on
Rhodes with bleached blond hair, looking like Gazza's kid
brother. It was time to restate the message that this was the
best young striker in Britain.

*I've never really changed as a person but I've learnt; I'm not really stupid in what I say now. I'm quite sensible. I'm not a bad lad anyway, full stop.*
**Robbie Fowler, FourFourTwo, 1996**

*I think I've started to grow up since those incidents. I'm not a bad lad but I want my exploits on the pitch to make headlines rather than the other stuff. I'm a young lad and enjoy having a bit of fun but I realise I'm in the public eye.*
**Robbie Fowler, The Mirror, 1996**

**IN THE NEXT SEASON,** Robbie was involved in an incident that turned him overnight into 'Honest Robbie'.

In a Liverpool v Arsenal clash in March 1997, as Fowler lanced forwards to pick up a pass, his fellow England international David Seaman came out and dived at Fowler's feet. Fowler tried to clear the approaching Seaman, but fell in the area, and referee Gerald Ashby awarded Liverpool a penalty.

In scenes unique in recent professional football history, Fowler protested to the referee that he had not been fouled. But all his pleas went unheeded, and the penalty stood. Fowler took it, and hit the post. Had justice been done? Jason McAteer wasn't bothered: he tapped the ball in off the rebound and beyond Seaman.

Reaction from Fowler's team-mates ranged from stunned incomprehension to faint praise indeed.

*I thought he was pleading with the referee not to send David Seaman off. It's usually the opposite, the striker asking for a penalty – I have never had this experience before.*
David James, *The Sun*, March 1997

*If Robbie felt he needed to do it, fair enough – but I can't say I would have done the same.*
Stan Collymore, *The Sun*, March 1997

**ELSEWHERE FOWLER** was praised widely for his actions, including a fax from the FIFA general secretary Sepp Blatter.

*Dear Robbie, I want to congratulate you for the act of sportsmanship which you demonstrated last evening in the match between Liverpool and Arsenal. It is the kind of gesture which helps maintain the integrity of the game.*
Sepp Blatter, March 1997

## GOD'S JOB'S A GOOD'UN

**THREE DAYS** AFTER RECEIVING the personal congratulations of FIFA's general secretary for his positive contribution to the beautiful game, Robbie was attracting the authorities' attention again, but this time he was back in their bad books.

UEFA slapped a £900 fine on him for lifting his shirt during a Cup Winners Cup tie to reveal a message on his T-shirt supporting the long-running Liverpool dockers strike. Fowler's concern was genuine: he knew many of the strikers personally, had grown up with them. It was a matter of local pride.

Robbie could at least take solace in the fact that his latest fine had been over a matter of conscience, rather than flashing his buttocks at opposing fans. And, as has been proved many a time, there has to be a touch of crankiness and passion in anyone who can regularly produce flashes of genius (n'est-ce pas, M. Cantona?).

After the glow of praise for his actions in querying the penalty decision against Arsenal, some more cynical voices weighed in with a less charitable approach, including Jimmy Greaves in his own open letter to the Liverpool striker:

*I'm not saying you dived – let's just say you took a very relaxed attitude to remaining upright. Then you realised, didn't you? Looked around at the faces of England team-*

*mates like David Seaman and Tony Adams and had a crisis of confidence. So you turned to the ref and told him it was all a mistake. No harm done. Let's forget it.*
Jimmy Greaves, *The Sun*, March 1997

*He has fire in his belly. He gets himself into trouble
with his mouthpiece.*
**Roy Evans**

**THE 1996-97** season had started in the hangover
of Euro 96, and for Robbie Fowler, it began with an
enforced break through injury, his first for two years.
The season also saw the start of a breakdown in the
excellent understanding which had grown up
between Fowler and Stan Collymore. This may have
resulted partly from Collymore's frustration at being
cast in the supporting role, even though he had
netted some superb strikes of his own.

*I played football for about two years non-stop. I had
a back injury and was not doing myself justice. Then
the ankle problem came along. I was struggling for a
while so maybe I needed the break. But I don't think
I played too much football. I love it. I get paid for it
and I am usually the last off the training pitch.*
**Robbie Fowler, The Sun, November 1996**

**RE-EMERGING** after his time on the
physiotherapist's table, Robbie revealed he had a
new regime. His penchant for Chinese take-aways
had been sidelined. His new diet was pasta: gnocchi
rather than noodles from now on. His alarm clock
was being set one hour earlier.

*I've followed what the dietician told me... Before I would feed on Chinese food six nights out of seven because I love it. It's a hardship to give it up but you have to make sacrifices if you want to feel better.*
Robbie Fowler, *The Mirror,* 1996

**AND HE** revealed what he really felt about the rigours of the training ground, where his new commitment to keeping in good physical shape would be scrutinised:

*I hate training. I prefer playing. I hate running. At Liverpool everyone's quite relaxed over training, but if you're not doing it in training they'll let you know and give you a bit of stick. And they'll make you do it. At Liverpool they say if you don't put it in in training, how do you expect to put it in during a match?*
Robbie Fowler, *FourFourTwo,* 1996

**IF THAT WAS** what ran through his mind, he managed to give the impression to others that training was *not* a problem.

*Pre-season training was always a breeze for him, he could do everything we asked. Most people hate running, but Robbie actually enjoys it.*
Steve Heighway, *The Observer*, 1996

**NOW THAT THE** relationship with Stan Collymore lacked the snap, crackle and pop of the previous season, and maybe because of the lingering after-effects of his injuries, Robbie was looking a touch out of sorts in front of goal, but nonetheless his tally continued to grow at a pace any other striker would have been proud of.

In December 1996, he reached a significant landmark in what was his 165th game for Liverpool. Needing two more goals to reach his century of strikes for the Reds, he potted a fantastic four in a 5-1 victory over relegation-bound Middlesbrough. The first came after a mere 29 seconds – Robbie's fastest goal ever for the club – but it was the second goal in the 28th minute, when he pounced on the rebound from a Collymore shot against the post that sent him and his fans into raptures as he racked up his 100th goal.

The Rush-Fowler comparison was immediately back in the news. Robbie had scored his 100th goal for Liverpool in one game fewer than the Welsh maestro.

*Robbie Fowler, like a batsman on song, went past his century with a four. It is a momentous feat, completed within a performance of irresistible team momentum. He is the poacher par excellence. When it mattered, his eye was keen, his balance superb, his execution infallible.*

Jeremy Alexander, *The Guardian*, 1996

**ROBBIE'S UNDERSHIRT** was becoming a mobile placard. After scoring the 100th goal, Robbie revealed a scrawled message on the T-shirt he was wearing underneath his Liverpool colours: 'God's job's a good'un.'

*A guy called Bez, who used to be in the Happy Mondays, now has his own TV show on Sundays and that is his catchphrase. I wanted to be wearing it on my shirt when I reached 100 goals.*

Robbie Fowler, *The Sun*, 1996

Robbie also told journalists that the pressure to beat Ian Rush's 100 goals in 166 games had been starting to get to him a little, so he was particularly relieved to have completed the deed.

*Rushie was Robbie's mentor. He will be pleased for the lad and can take a great deal of credit from this himself.*

Roy Evans, *The Sun*, 1996

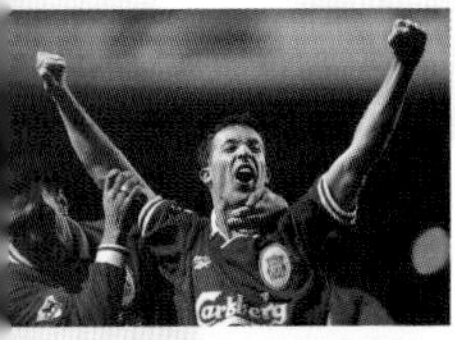

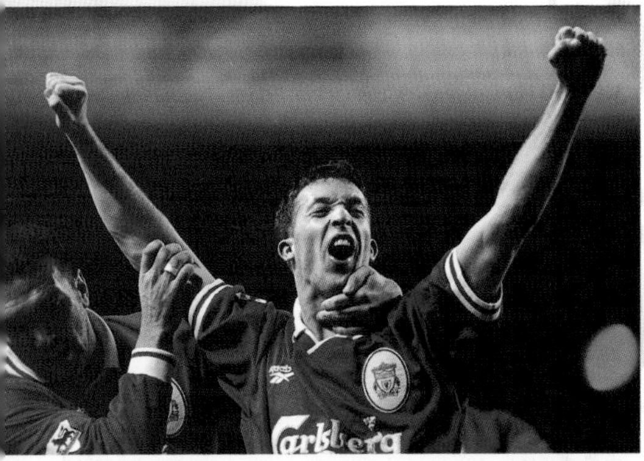

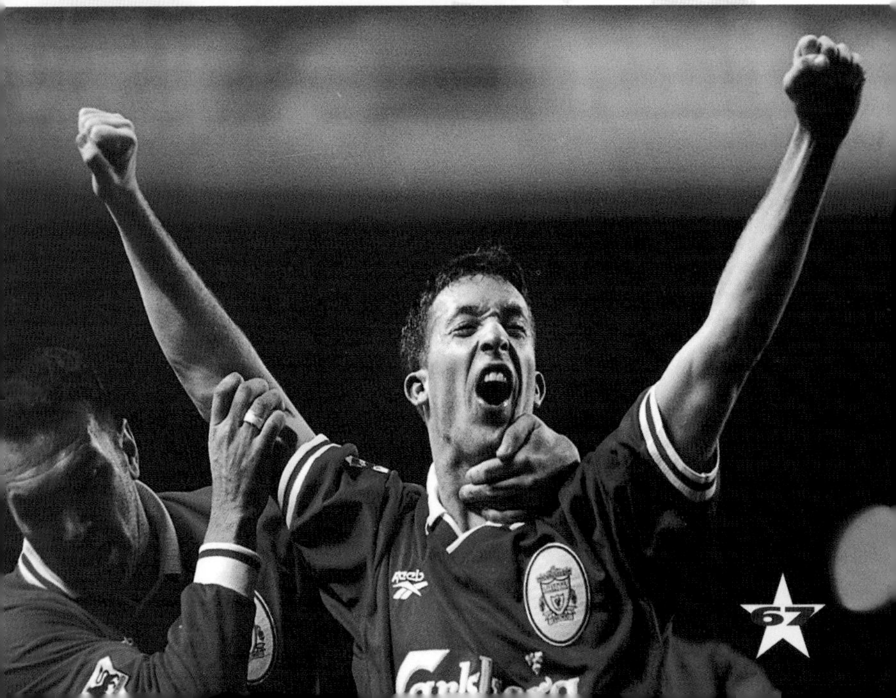

## MIXED FORTUNES

**IN ENGLAND'S** OPENING qualifiers for the 1998 World Cup in France, under new England coach Glenn Hoddle, Robbie had failed to appear even as substitute. But Hoddle brought him back later in the season for a Wembley friendly against Mexico on 30 March 1997; a match which gave Robbie his sixth cap, another full start, and – most significantly of all – his first international goal.

He was paired upfront with Arsenal's Ian Wright, and it was the Highbury hitman who provided Fowler with the opportunity he had been waiting for. A Wright header was blocked, and as the attempt rebounded, Robbie ran on to the loose ball to put it away. The Gunners' striker realised just how much it meant for his strike partner – he had had to wait eight games before getting his own debut international goal.

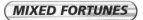

*To get a goal so early on in your career like Robbie has just done is an important breakthrough. He can now go on and score goals for us for the next 10 years.*
Ian Wright, *The Sun*, 1996

*I tried not to think about anything other than England. I did not feel pressure.*
*Whenever I go out to play I only think about two things, winning and scoring. It was the same this time.*
Robbie Fowler, *The Sun*, 1996

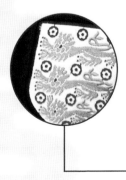

**STILL ONLY TWENTY-ONE,** Robbie had opened a new account ledger at the top level. But his international career took a wrong turn only three months later, when Liverpool refused to release Fowler (and Steve McManaman) for international duties. He would be unavailable for a World Cup qualifier against Poland and Le Tournoi, the four-team competition which featured England, alongside Brazil, Italy and France.

The reason given for Fowler's absence was that he needed an operation on his nose. Nobody was questioning whether or not Robbie required the surgery, but what seemed unnecessary was the timing. Certainly Glenn Hoddle was distinctly under-impressed to say the least and gave out very strong signals that this would have an adverse effect on Robbie's future career with the national team.

When England ran out as comfortable winners of Le Tournoi (added to their impressive performance against Poland), continuing to establish themselves as a genuinely potent force in the world game, the decision by Fowler's Anfield advisers seemed to be particularly unfortunate.

And when, later that summer, England's number one pick Alan Shearer was badly injured in one of Newcastle's pre-season matches and seemed likely to be out of action for some key internationals, it seemed doubly so. At a time when the biggest arena of all was beckoning, Robbie might find himself completely out of the reckoning.

By the end of the 1996-97 season, a comparatively disappointing one for Liverpool; unable to prevent a Cantona-less Manchester United stride towards yet another Premiership title and failing to pick up a major trophy, Robbie had managed his third consecutive tally of 30-plus goals, ending as joint top scorer. He had now made 140 League appearances for the club, and scored 83 League goals – an impressive, and invaluable, strike rate of nearly 0.6 goals per game.

His international prospects might have dimmed, but his domestic success was still buoyant, and he had been able to put his healthy earnings potential to good use.

True to his Toxteth roots he had bought his own house not far from the massive Anglican cathedral in Liverpool, eschewing the successful professional's traditional move away from the city, into the suburbs and beyond.

He also bought a house for his mother – his parents are separated. There was an obvious affection for both his parents, and traces of a good upbringing lingered into adult life.

*He's an odd one is Fowler. A self-professed 'mummy's boy', he looks coy when he speaks, almost Di-like shy at times. And he's terribly well-mannered, offering the photographer and myself one of his sandwiches and guiltily wiping chocolate off his fingers as he munches through a long-awaited chocolate-chip cookie.*
Karen Buchanan, *FourFourTwo,* 1996

*I've bought my mum a new house. It was brilliant. Ever since I was little I said to my mum I would buy her a house if I made it. I'll get my dad a house soon. He's never asked me to buy him one, but I will.*
Robbie Fowler, *Total Football,* 1995

**IN HIS TIME OFF** he would still go and hang out with the mates he had known as a kid. The hot-headedness of his first few years had been the natural exuberance of an average lad – he had just had to do his growing up in a very public eye. Keeping close to family and friends helped to keep his feet on the ground.

*We're a down-to-earth family and they make sure I do the right things. Anyway, if I ever did get big-headed, my dad would soon put me down. He's watched every game I've played since I was 11 and knows when to put me in my place.*
Robbie Fowler, *The Mirror,* 1996

*I still keep in touch with all my mates whether it be from school or friends from out of school. I'm still the same person.*
Robbie Fowler, *Total Football,* 1995

**DURING THE 1996-97** season, Robbie had flirted with the world of the tabloid gossip columns and *Hello!* magazine when he made a large number of grown men extremely jealous by dating Emma Bunton, Baby Spice. The football and music industries had usually – and thankfully – concentrated on what they were good at, with crossover restricted to the annually excruciating FA Cup singles. But in the afterglow of 'Three Lions On The Shirt', the new, youthful pop and soccer aristocracies seemed to be forming their own dynasty. Manchester United's David Beckham was squiring Posh Spice, Victoria Adams, around town. Robbie's clubmate Jamie Redknapp was seeing ex-Eternal star Louise, voted the UK's sexiest woman. The Liverpool team found itself dubbed the Spice Boys. But you couldn't help feeling that Robbie was most comfortable enjoying a pint in a Liverpool pub.

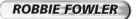
## *THE FUTURE IS BRIGHT*

**DESPITE THE** CLOUD HANGING over his international career, Robbie's contribution to the 1997-98 season was awaited eagerly. Stan Collymore had departed to Aston Villa – he had been a vital element in the Toxteth Terror's continued success, as a support-Fowler goal-machine. If Fowler could find an equally talented and selfless feed, he could confidently set about achieving his next target, pursuing his 200th goal for Liverpool.

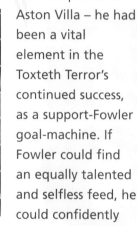

Further down the line was Ian Rush's Liverpool League goal total of 233 goals, 12 shy of Roger Hunt's 245 League goals scored between 1959 and 1969.

Time at least was on his

side. He had started in the full Liverpool team as an 18-year-old. If he avoided the injury problems that were the bane of the professional's life, and if his appetite for goalscoring remained as sharp as ever, he would have every chance of breaking those records.

Still only 22 years old, Robbie's financial future was secure. On a reported £10,000 a week contract, and with one endorsement contract, a five-year deal for Nike football boots, rumoured to be worth £3 million pounds, he was set to become one of the sport's big earners. It seemed he had no desire to leave his second home, Anfield, for one of the other Premiership giants or for foreign pastures.

*At the moment I'm well happy at Liverpool. I would love to stay all my life. People talk about Manchester United or Arsenal, but Liverpool have been on top for 30 or 40 years. I reckon with the side we've got we can be on top for the next 10 years. At least.*

**Robbie Fowler,** *Total Football,* **1995**

**HE WAS** also well aware of the theories expounded on the maturing of soccer players and that, according to one such opinion, he still had a full five years to go before he reached his best.

*I remember years ago I used to watch Everton and somebody in the crowd said professional footballers don't necessarily reach their peak until they're 27. I hope it's true. I don't know if it's true or not.*
Robbie Fowler, *FourFourTwo*, 1996

**ONE REASON** he was happy at Liverpool was the team spirit amongst the players at the core of the team, even if they didn't all have as strong a local credibility as Robbie himself.

*We've got a lot of Cockneys in the team, but really, it doesn't matter where they're from – we're all playing for Liverpool.*
Robbie Fowler, *Total Football*, 1995

**ONE SUCH LONDONER** was 'Razor' Ruddock, who had his own suitable nickname for his clubmate.

*Robbie Fowler is the Artful Dodger. The Dodger used to pinch stuff out of people's pockets – Robbie pinches goals from defences.*
Neil Ruddock, *The Sun*, August 1994

**ALONGSIDE THE DODGER,** Ruddock revealed, were
Shaggy (Steve McManaman), Trigger (Rob Jones) and God
(Jamie Redknapp – although this was also a Kop nickname for
Robbie). It was a sign of the good spirit that existed at the
heart of the team – apart from when Razor and the Dodger
were having a little spat at the occasional airport – and which
would be there to carry through to the 1997-98 squad.

If Robbie could ride the intensity of press interest in his
professional and private life, he would be able to poach more
than just a pocket or two. He just had to stop the pressures
getting to him.

*When Ian Rush first started he was a brilliant player, of
course, but there can't have been as much attention focussed
on him. That gave him time to grow up out of the limelight.
Now you only have to look at what Ryan Giggs has to put up
with to see what I'm talking about. I feel sorry for him.*
**Robbie Fowler, *The Mirror*, 1996**

**HIS MANY ADMIRERS** had no such doubts that the Flying Scouseman would deliver with plenty to spare.

*Many thought they'd never see the like of Ian Rush again. But while Robbie Fowler has yet to match the longevity of his mentor, he's shown enough to suggest that it'll be the new Fowler they're looking for in ten years' time.*

Tommy Docherty, *FourFourTwo*, 1997

*Sometimes, just occasionally, football presents us with a player of such immense natural ability, and the will to apply it, that we can only sit back in admiration and hope those who make the game's big decisions make the most of it.*
**John Sadler, *The Sun*, 1996**

*If Fowler seems simple, that's because he is. Simple, uncomplicated, instinctive. On the pitch and off it. Fowler is the fan who's been given a chance to play. He's not going to argue with it or attempt to define it. He's just a lad doing a job.*
**Karen Buchanan, *FourFourTwo*, 1996**

*Robbie has a rare talent. You cannot teach it, you cannot coach it. He just has it.*
**Roy Evans**

*I hate talking about football. I just do it, you know?*
**Robbie Fowler, *FourFourTwo*, 1996**

## FACT FILE

- *Full Name*:
  Robert Fowler
- *Height*:
  5'8"
- *Weight*:
  11st 10lb
- *Born*:
  9 April 1975 in Liverpool, England
- *Career*:
  Spotted by **Liverpool** scout. YTS Trainee for Liverpool. Turned professional in April 1992.

### FOWLER'S GOLDEN MOMENTS

- Scored 5 goals in second leg of 1st round of Coca-Cola Cup v Fulham September 1993 – only the fourth player in Liverpool's history to do so.

- Scored first League hat-trick v Southampton in only his fifth League game.
- 12 goals in his first 13 senior appearances for Liverpool.
- An FA disrepute charge after an incident at Filbert Street during a game v Leicester. Subsequently fined 1,000.
- 1994-95 season Robbie was the first Anfield player in six years to top 30 goals (31).
- Named Professional Football Association's Young Player of the Year (1994-95).
- Constantly compared with the arch goal-poacher Jimmy Greaves.

## ROBBIE'S GOALS
- Finished 1993-94 season with 18 goals (leading Liverpool scorer that season).
- Scored five goals in the first three League games of 1994-95.
- Scored fastest ever hat-trick in the Premiership v Arsenal – (in just 4 minutes 32 seconds.
- Finished 1994-95 season with 31 goals (25 League, 4 Coca-Cola Cup, 2 FA Cup). Again was Liverpool's highest goal scorer.
- Robbie completed 1995-96 with 36 goals despite the fact that he had been left out of the side at the beginning of the season in favour of Rush and Collymore.
- By the end of 1996-97 season, Fowler's score totalled 83 goals for his team.

## ROBBIE THE INTERNATIONAL
- England Youth team and England Under-21 squad.
- Played first game v San Marino November 1993 and scored in three minutes!
- Sent off in November 1994 during an international game for the England Under-21s against Austria. Robbie was suspended for 4 games by UEFA.
- First full England cap against Croatia.
- 6 full England caps.

## LIVERPOOL
- Ground: Anfield Road, Liverpool L4 0TH.
- Ground capacity: 35,000 (by February 1998, there will be room for 45,000 supporters).
- Pitch measurements: 111yd x 74yd.
- Date formed: 15 March 1892.
- Previous name: Liverpool Association FC.
  Nicknames: 'Reds'; 'Pool'.
- Current sponsors: Carlsberg.
- Greatest rivals: Formerly Everton, but now Manchester United
- Celebrity fans: Ian Brodie, Sporty Spice, Stan Boardman & Jimmy Tarbuck.
- Weirdest merchandise: Life-size Robbie Fowlers to keep the creases in your clothes.
- Fan's favourite: Robbie Fowler.
- It's True: The first Liverpool side had ten Scots players and an English goalie.
- Management history: George Kay 1935-51; Don Welsh 1951-56; Phil Taylor 1956-59; Bill Shankly 1959-74; Bob Paisley 1974-83; Joe Fagan 1983-85; Kenny Daglish 1985-91; Graeme Souness 1991-94; Roy Evans 1994 onwards.
- Greatest score: 11-0 v Stromsgodset - European Cup Winners' Cup 17 September 1979.
- Record defeat: 1-9 v Birmingham City Division 2 11 December 1954.
- Leading goalscorers:
  *Then*: Ian Rush 47 goals
  (32 League; 2 FA Cup; 8 League Cup; 5 European Cup)
  *Now*: Robbie Fowler 31 goals (18 League; 7 European Cup Winners' Cup; 5 League Cup; 1 FA Cup).
- Record Transfer paid: £7 million for Stan Collymore from Aston Villa (June 1997).
- Record Transfer received: £8.5 million for Stan Collymore from Nottingham Forest (July 1995).

- Record attendance: 61,905 v Wolverhampton Wanderers FA Cup 4th Round 2 February 1952
- Club Honours:
  Division One
  1900-1, 1905-6, 1921-22, 1922-23, 1946-7, 1963-64, 1965-66, 1972-73, 1975-76, 1976-77, 1978-79, 1981-82, 1982-83, 1983-84, 1985-86, 1987-88, 1989-90.
  Division Two
  1893-94, 1895-96, 1904-5, 1961-62.
  FA Cup Winners
  1964-65, 1973-74, 1985-86, 1988-89, 1991-92.
  League Cup
  1980-81, 1981-82, 1982-83, 1983-84, 1994-95.
  European Cup
  1976-77, 1977-78, 1980-81, 1983-84.
  UEFA Cup 1972-73, 1975-76.
  European Super Cup 1977.
  League Super Cup 1986.

- Best website: http://anfield.merseyworld.com/ (unofficial). Liverpool do not have an official website at the moment.
- Liverpool FC came about because of a dispute between Everton, who were resident at Anfield Road, and the landlord, Mr John Houlding. The dispute happened in 1892 and most of the players quit the ground to begin at Goodison Park. As a result, John Houlding formed a new team to play at his ground. Liverpool was born.
- Liverpool boast three of the greatest goalkeepers of all time in Sam Hardy, Elisha Scott and Billy Liddell.
- Heavyweight boxer Joe Louis signed for Liverpool in 1944, but he never played a game for them.

- 1959 heralded the arrival of Bill Shankly who took the Division Two side into the First Division and then on to 3 championship wins, 2 FA Cup wins and the UEFA Cup.
- Shankly drew the big names to Liverpool including Ray Clemence, Emlyn Hughes, Roger Hunt, Kevin Keegan, Tommy Smith, Ian St John, John Toshack & Ron Yeats.
- In the 1961-62 season Liverpool were in Division Two. During that time, Roger Hunt scored 41 League goals.

- Bob Paisley took over in 1974 as Liverpool dominated the football scene for nearly two decades. He signed Kenny Dalglish and Graeme Souness.
- On 17 September 1974, Liverpool beat Stromsgodset Drammen 11-0.
- Liverpool lifted the UEFA Cup for a second time in 1976.
- Liverpool became only the second English side to win the European Cup in 1977, they beat Borussia Moechengladbach 3-1.
- 1982-83 Bob Paisley left Anfield after 43 years. He managed to help Liverpool secure 13 trophies, including 3 European Cups, 6 League Championships, 3 Milk Cups & the UEFA Cup.
- In 1983-84 Joe Fagan took over at Anfield. Under his guidance, Liverpool made the big play for the treble; Ian Rush scored five goals against Luton; Brentford dropped out of the Milk Cup with eight goals (on aggregate); Liverpool met and beat Everton in the final and lifted the Milk Cup for a record fourth time.
- 1985 Heysel Stadium disaster.
- Kenny Dalglish took Liverpool to the double.
- 1989 Hillsborough Stadium tragedy.

- In June 1995, Liverpool paid their record transfer fee of £8,500,000 to Nottingham Forest for Stan Collymore.
- When Stan Collymore was transferred to Aston Villa in May 1997, Liverpool received £7 million.
- On 12 September 1996, Liverpool scored a 1-0 win over MyPa-47 in the first round of the Cup Winners' Cup in Finland.
- 15 September 1996, Liverpool went to the top of the Premiership by 2 pts (the result of a 3-0 victory at Leicester).
- Five year Premiership record up to 1996-97: 4th, 3rd, 4th, 8th & 6th.
- After Steve McManaman's aborted transfer to Barcelona for £12 million, Roy Evans hopes that the English winger will remain with Liverpool.
- The last five years have been the worst in the club's history in terms of major wins, but they have still managed to grab both of the domestic cups.
- The most capped player in Liverpool's history is Ian Rush with 67 caps for Wales.

## CURRENT LIVERPOOL SQUAD

- Goalkeepers: David James (English, England international, England B, Under-21 & Youth) previous club Watford. Signed for £1million Tony Warner (English). Signed as a Trainee. Jorgen Nielsen (Danish Under-21).
- Defenders Rob Jones (English with 8 caps) previous club Crewe Alexandra. Bjorn Tore Kvarme (Norwegian) previous club Rosenborg (free transfer). Mark Wright (45 caps) previous clubs Oxford United, Southampton & Derby County. Signed for £2.2m. Phil Babb (Republic of Ireland with 20 caps) previous clubs Millwall, Bradford City & Coventry. Signed for £3.6m. Steve Harkness (English)

previous clubs Carlisle, Huddersfield Town (loan) and Southend United (loan). Neil Ruddock (English international with 1 cap) previous clubs Millwall, Tottenham Hotspur and Southampton. Stig-Inge Bjornebye (Norwegian international with 52 caps) previous club Rosenborg. Signed for a bargain at £600,000. Dominic Matteo (English Under-21 with 3 caps). Signed as a Trainee, but loaned to Sunderland.

- Midfielders/Wingers/Wing-backs: Jason McAteer (Republic of Ireland international) previous club Bolton Wanderers. Steve McManaman (English international). Oyvind Leonhardson (Norwegian international with 52 caps) previous clubs Rosenborg & Wimbledon. Signed for £3.5 million from Wimbledon (they paid Rosenborg only £300,000). Jamie Redknapp (English international with 5 caps) previous club Bournemouth. Patrick Berger (Czech international) previous clubs Sparta Prague, Slavia Prague and Borussia Dortmund. Michael Thomas (English) previous clubs Arsenal & Portsmouth (loan). Signed for £1.5 million. Paul Ince (English international) previous clubs West Ham United, Manchester United & Internazionale. Signed for £4.25 million. Joe Carragher (English). Signed as a Trainee. Danny Murphy (English) previous club Crewe Alexandra for £1.5 million (although delayed as Danny has a knee injury).

- Forwards: Robbie Fowler (English international). Karlheinz Reidle (German international with 42 caps) previous clubs Blau-Weiss Berlin, Werder Bremen, Lazio, Borussia Dortmund. Signed for £1.75 million. Michael Owen (Republic of Ireland international with 10 caps) previous club Millwall. Signed for £1.5 million. David Thompson (English Youth and Under-21) signed up as a Trainee.

- Who's Bad? Jason McAteer & Mark Wright with seven yellow cards last season.

- One to watch: Michael Owen.

Introduction by Robert Jeffery.
Robert Jeffery worked on local newspapers before helping to launch *Sky Sports Magazine*. He is currently a reporter on *FourFourTwo*, Britain's best-selling football magazine. He supports Wimbledon and Slough Town.

Main text by Philip Dodd.
Philip Dodd is a writer and publishing consultant specialising in popular culture, including sport and music. In 1996, he was the publisher of *The Virgin Book of Football Records*. He is a lifelong supporter of Ipswich Town, through the good times and the bad.

Fact file compiled by Jon Sutherland.

The Foundry would like to thank Helen Burke, Helen Courtney, Helen Johnson, Lucinda Hawksley, Lee Matthews, Morse Modaberi and Sonya Newland for all their work on this project.

Picture Credits
All pictures © copyright Empics Sports Photo Agency